The Celts

Contents

Written by Sean Callery

Illustrations by Arpad Olbey

Collins

Where did the Celts come from?

The word "Celt" describes a group of many different tribes that lived across much of Europe over 2,000 years ago, during the Iron Age (800 BCE–43 CE).

They didn't actually call themselves Celts. The word wasn't used to describe them until about 1770, and it's still used today. It comes from the Greek word *Keltoi*, which means barbarians and describes people not from Rome or Greece.

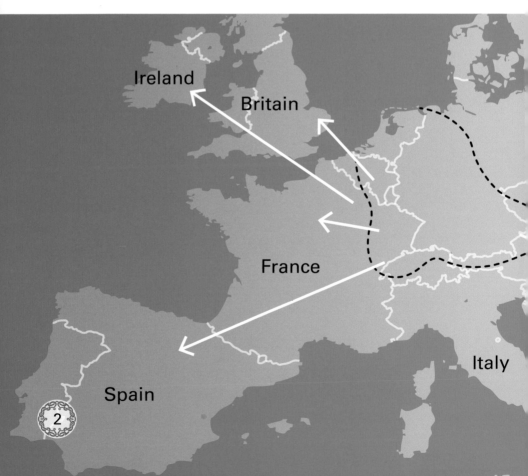

The people we call Iron Age Celts lived in modern-day France, Spain and northern Italy. By 500 BCE, the tribes had **migrated** – some went east, to modern-day Turkey, and others moved west, to Britain. They spoke a Celtic language, and introduced it to Britain when the tribes migrated.

Key:
- – – – early Celtic area
←——— Celtic expansion

some Celts
went east

Turkey

Making a home

Britain was a land of forests and wide rivers. The people who lived there farmed and hunted and may have formed tribes. To the people arriving from Europe, Britain wouldn't have been very different from where they had come.

Once they arrived in Britain, Iron Age Celts built their houses from whatever materials they could find. In the forests of Britain, houses were built with wood, with walls made of clay, animal hair and straw. On the wild upland moors of Cornwall and Scotland houses were built with stone.

Houses were round, and had one large room inside. A cooking pot hung over the central open fire that kept the house warm. The smoke escaped through the thatched roof made from reeds or straw. The floor was flattened earth covered with animal skins or straw.

The whole family lived together, so as many as 20 people might sleep in each house.

cooking inside the roundhouse

cooking pot

central fire

a reconstruction of a roundhouse

Defending the home

Some houses were built over water. Long wooden poles were transported by boat into the river or **loch**. They were then driven into the water using smaller, heavier pieces of wood. A wooden platform was built on top, and then the roundhouse.

Houses like these were called crannogs, and they were built like this to protect the people who lived there from attack.

Over 600 crannogs have been found in Scotland. Others have been found in Wales and **Scandinavia**.

wooden poles supporting the house

a hill fort

The Iron Age Celts also built forts on the top of hills to protect the people living in nearby villages. They also contained storerooms and cattle enclosures. These are called hill forts.

Huge mounds of earth were piled up around a hill, and wooden walls were built on top of them. This meant that attackers could be seen coming, and spears and rocks could be fired at them from above. One hill fort had a pit with more than 20,000 pebbles gathered from the seashore to launch at enemies.

Warriors

At that time, most people only lived until they were 35 to 40 years old. Some warriors may not have even lived that long.

Warriors were important members of Iron Age Celtic society. They protected the village from attack. They may have also stolen goods, animals or food from other villages.

When two tribes fought for land, warriors would begin the battle by blowing trumpets, pipes, drums and yelling. Then they would race their two-horse chariots straight at the enemy, throwing spears. Once they had reached the enemy, they would climb out of the chariot and attack on foot with swords, using their shields to protect themselves.

Warriors painted or **tattooed** patterns on to their bodies using blue dye. This would have made them look scary, and the Iron Age Celts may have believed the patterns gave them protection.

Warriors cut off dead enemies' heads and took them home to display.

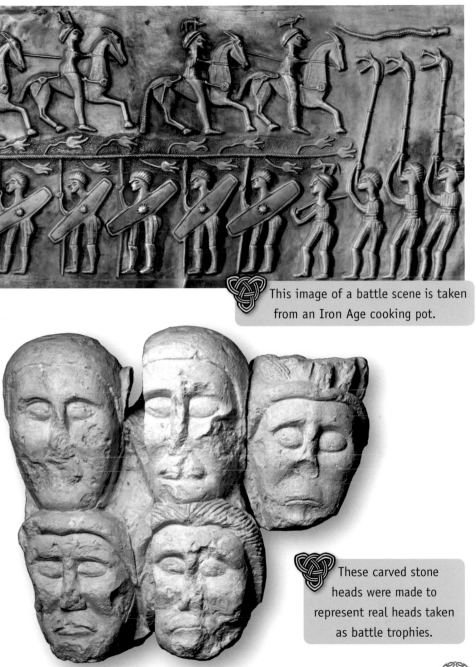

This image of a battle scene is taken from an Iron Age cooking pot.

These carved stone heads were made to represent real heads taken as battle trophies.

Into battle

Iron Age people knew how to make armour and weapons – they were well equipped for war!

War trumpets were made of brass and bronze. They had a long tube so that the sound would travel over people's heads and make the warriors feel brave and ready for battle.

the mouth of a trumpet, shaped like an animal head

The armour worn by warriors included bronze helmets, sometimes decorated with feathers, horse tails or animal horns. Chain-mail shirts were also worn, but probably only by very important people as these would have taken a long time to make.

Daggers, swords, spears, slings, shields and axes were all used by warriors. They would have defended themselves with a shield made of wood, strengthened with iron and covered in leather.

a richly decorated Iron Age sword

Women's rights

Boys *and* girls were trained to use swords, and women could become warriors, fight in battles and lead a tribe. In fact, women had much more freedom and power in Iron Age Celtic society than in Ancient Greece or Rome. Married couples shared their possessions equally, and women could have many of the same jobs as men.

One of the most famous female warriors and tribal leaders is Boudica, who ruled the Iceni tribe in modern-day East Anglia, England.

Farmers first

When they weren't fighting, the Iron Age Celts farmed.
They were expert farmers – they had to be to stay alive.
They used ploughs, which were pulled across fields
by oxen in a criss-cross pattern to break up the soil.
This meant that they could grow crops, such as barley,
wheat and oats, over large areas. They used iron tools,
like **scythes**, and wheeled carts and equipment to
harvest crops.

Barley and wheat were crushed between two large stones, and the flour made into bread. The Iron Age Celts ate a lot of beans, and possibly parsnips and cabbages. They hunted wild boar, collected nuts and berries, and may have also fished. Their diet would have changed through the year as crops ripened.

Children did jobs to help out. They cleared weeds, fetched water, helped with the harvest, and looked after animals.

Animals such as hens, sheep and cows were kept for meat, eggs, wool and leather. Cows and sheep also gave milk, which was turned into butter and cheese.

Most food was cooked in a large pot that hung over the fire, probably as stews. Food was sometimes cooked in outside ovens in the summer.

thatched roof

central hearth

flattened earth floor

It was important to make sure there was a food supply throughout the year. Meat was **preserved** by rubbing it with salt or by hanging it over a smoky fire. This meant it didn't go rotten. Grain was stored in underground pits lined with stone or **wicker** and sealed with clay to keep it dry.

Iron Age Celts kept bees and the wax was used to make candles. There was no sugar, so honey was used to sweeten food. They made a drink out of hops or barley, which everyone drank, including the children.

 Decorated horns like this were sometimes used to drink from.

Colourful clothes

The Iron Age Celts made their clothing out of wool and linen. They used a large wooden machine called a loom to weave the wool into cloth, which was patterned and brightly coloured using dyes. The dyes were made from trees, plants and animals: blue colours from the leaves of a plant known as woad, brown from oak bark and greens from **lichen**. In parts of Europe, insects called cochineal were crushed to make red dye.

They also wore animal hides, which they preserved by rubbing with salt, and hanging over a smoky fire. Men wore trousers, which was unusual at the time (Romans wore robes). Women wore long, loose **tunics** and dresses. Iron Age Celts may have worn their hair long, with gold and glass hair beads.

Celtic clothes didn't have buttons. Instead, they used pins or brooches made in **intricate** designs.

a decorated bronze brooch

Crafts

As well as making clothes, Iron Age Celts knew how to work with different materials such as wood, clay, glass, iron, bronze, gold and silver.

Clay was made into everyday items such as pots and jugs.

Wood was carved into tools and sculptures.

Metals were made into jewellery such as arm bands, ankle rings and torcs – a twisted coil worn around

a pottery jug

the neck, made of valuable metal like gold. Jewellery like this would have been worn by important people.

a torc

20

One metalworking method the Celts used was called "lost wax" casting. Spear heads were made this way, and then attached to wooden poles.

1. A shape was carved into a lump of beeswax.

2. The finished shape was wrapped in clay.

3. The clay was heated up so that the beeswax melted and was poured out.

4. Hot metal was poured into the clay mould, then left to cool.

5. The clay mould was broken open, to reveal the finished metal object.

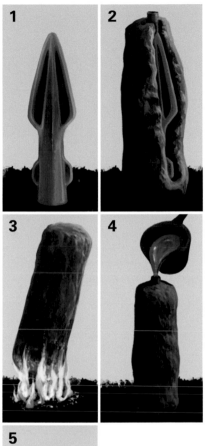

Traders

The Iron Age Celts traded the crafts that they'd made with each other, and with neighbours across and beyond Europe. Early in the Iron Age they would have **bartered** things like leather made from the skins of their cattle, hunting dogs and jewellery. They also bartered materials they had dug out of underground mines, such as salt and tin.

Much later in the Iron Age, coins may have been exchanged for goods.

These coins are from the 1st century CE. They show the earliest example of writing in Iron Age Britain – the name of a British king called Tincomarus.

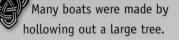

Many boats were made by hollowing out a large tree.

Traders travelled from Britain to modern-day France in boats made of wood, possibly covered in animal skins. These boats had sails, and wooden paddles were used to push the vessel at speed through the water.

The traders brought back wine and olive oil from the Romans.

This is a log raft, which would have been used to transport goods and people on lakes and rivers.

Entertainment

Traders weren't the only people to travel. Performers, known as bards, travelled from place to place. They would tell stories, poems and sing songs. At that time people couldn't read or write so the stories would change over the years.

Iron Age Celts also entertained themselves by playing flutes, small harps, drums, bagpipes and violins. These instruments were made of wood, bone and animal skin. Some of them looked very similar to instruments played today.

Adults and children may have played board games. Dice were made from bones and counters made from glass, wood, metal or pottery. They may also have played shooting games with marbles made from coloured stone.

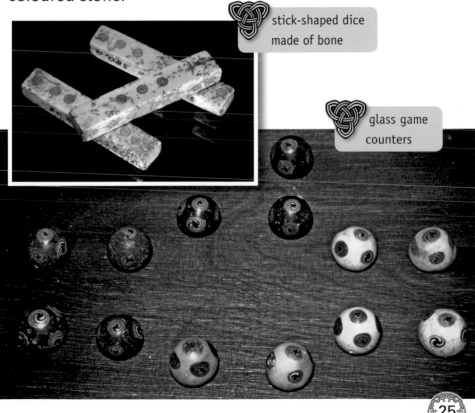

stick-shaped dice made of bone

glass game counters

Many gods

Some of the bards' tales were about the gods. The Iron Age Celts believed in a family of gods and goddesses who controlled the world around them.

Some gods and goddesses were linked to the landscape such as Artio, goddess of the forest. Others had greater powers, such as Taranis, the god of the heavens (also known as the thunder god) and Camulos, god of war. Powerful female goddesses include Danu, the mother goddess.

Brigit, the goddess of new life

Cernunnos, a god usually shown with antlers or horns

Epona, the goddess of horses

Maponos, the
god of youth

The number three was special to the Iron Age Celts.
They pictured their gods with three heads, and often
gave them three names. This may be because they
saw the world as made up of three things: earth, sea
and air.

27

Festivals

Four important festivals were celebrated. Each festival was linked to a particular god and what was happening on the farm.

Date	1 November	1 February
Festival name	Samhain	Imbolc
Key god	Samhain god of the dead	Brigit, goddess of new life
Event	The start of the year. The Celts believed the spirits of the dead visited them.	Lighting of candles.
Farm event	The cattle were brought in from the fields.	Sheep started to give birth.

1 May	1 August
Beltane	Lugnasad
Belenos, the sun god	Lugh, god of harvest and crafts
Bonfires burned on hills.	The first cut of corn was burned.
Cattle were driven through smoke to kill pests, then put in the fields.	The harvest began.

Sacrifices

The Iron Age Celts **sacrificed** people and animals to please the gods. Priests, called druids, were in charge of these sacrifices.

In later times, the Celts only sacrificed animals, rather than people, but experts don't know why this change occurred.

Iron Age Celts also tried to please their gods by offering them their most precious things. Water was seen as a pathway to the gods, so they threw special objects like shields, swords and jewellery into rivers, lakes and even wells.

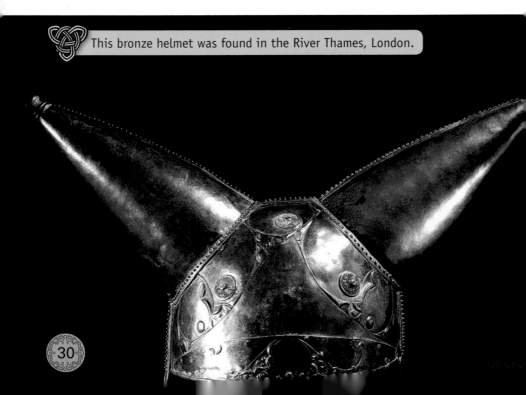

This bronze helmet was found in the River Thames, London.

Like the helmet, this bronze shield was not sturdy
enough to be used in battle, but may
have been made especially for the gods.

Burials

Experts know lots about the Iron Age Celts from objects offered to the gods, and also from the things they buried with their dead. The Iron Age Celts believed in an afterlife and they wanted their loved ones to have possessions in the next world.

Rich people were buried with valuable gold objects such as daggers, jewellery, even whole wagons. Poor people were buried with fewer objects. There aren't many images of people from the Iron Age – most of the images created by crafts people were just patterns. But some buckets have been found in burials with decorated faces in bronze.

a face decoration on
a bronze cauldron

The way the Iron Age Celts buried their dead changed in different places and at different times. In Europe, bodies were buried underground. In Britain, they were left in the open air until the body rotted away, and then the bones were buried. From about 100 CE, Iron Age Celts throughout Europe started to burn their dead and bury the ashes.

Archaeologists found weapons and jewellery in the grave of this Celtic woman.

The fall of the Iron Age Celts in Europe

The Iron Age Celts' way of life didn't last. The Romans, who had an army with better weapons and training, took over lands occupied by the Iron Age Celts in Europe.

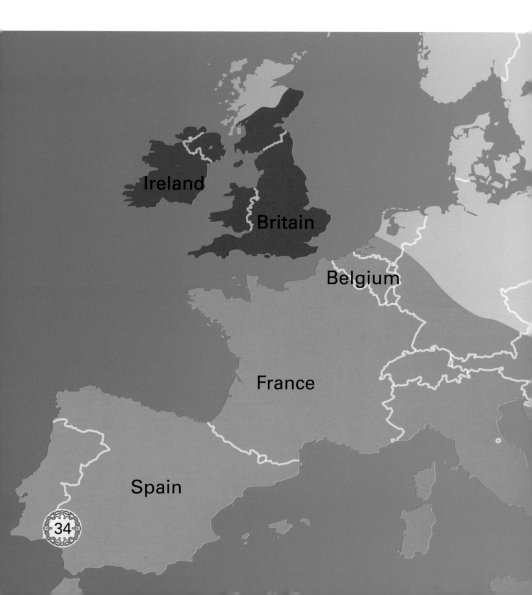

Ireland

Britain

Belgium

France

Spain

Although tribes of Iron Age Celts attacked and occupied Rome for seven months in 390 BCE, the Romans fought back and by 200 BCE the Roman army controlled much of the land in Europe.

Iron Age Celtic tribes survived in isolated places such as Britain, but that didn't last.

Key:
Roman territory
Remaining Celt territory

Turkey

The end of the Iron Age Celts in Britain

In 55–54 BCE Julius Caesar tried to **conquer** Britain.
He sailed with about 12,000 men across the English
Channel but the Iron Age Celts defeated them.
Caesar did try to conquer Britain a second time, with
an army of 30,000 men, but was again unsuccessful.

a statue of Julius
Caesar in Rome

Nearly 100 years after Julius Caesar tried to invade, the Roman Emperor Claudius sent an army to Britain. A large force of 40,000 Roman soldiers successfully took control of the southern half of Britain. They allowed some of the tribal leaders to stay, as long as they paid **taxes** to Rome.

Not all the Iron Age Celtic tribes wanted to be ruled by the Romans. In 60 CE Boudica led a **rebellion** against the invaders. The Iceni tribe destroyed the key Roman towns of Colchester, London and St Albans, but she was finally defeated by the Romans a year later, in 61 CE.

The Iron Age Celts were seen as such a threat by the Romans that one Roman emperor, Hadrian, built a wall across northern Britain to keep them out. This was one of the events that led to the creation of modern-day Scotland.

The Romans left Britain 300 later, in 380 CE. When the Angles and Saxons arrived from Norway, Sweden and Denmark 20 years later, in about 400 CE, many of the remaining Iron Age Celts in Britain moved westwards, to modern-day Cornwall, Wales and Ireland, and north to modern-day Scotland. They never dominated Britain again.

 Much of Hadrian's Wall in the north of England can still be seen today.

Iron Age Celtic culture lives on

Is there anything left of Iron Age Celtic culture today?

The Gaelic languages of Ireland, Scotland, **Manx**, Welsh, Cornish and **Breton** all came from the Iron Age Celts.

Iron Age Celtic designs had a big influence on later art. They are full of intricate curved patterns, often with animals or faces hidden into the designs. A typical Celtic design is the knot work, which looks like a braided strip.

The defences that Iron Age Celts constructed, like hill forts, can still be seen today, even though the wood that the fences were built with has rotted away.

Many figures and animals carved into chalk hills by the Iron Age Celts can still be seen today. These may have been carved to mark territory, or as an offering to the gods.

This white horse is cut into a chalk hillside at Uffington in Oxfordshire. It can be seen for miles.

The Romans wrote a lot about the Iron Age Celts, but the best information about these people has come from found objects. Weapons like swords, shields – even fragments of cloth and wood. These items tell us how the Iron Age Celts successfully made a home in Britain for hundreds of years, and why their culture lives on.

Glossary

BCE	stands for before the common era
CE	stands for the common era
bartered	goods of similar value swapped without the use of money
Breton	Celtic language spoken in Brittany, France
conquer	take over by force
intricate	very complicated or detailed
lichen	type of plant
loch	Scottish name for a lake
Manx	Celtic language spoken on the Isle of Man
migrated	moved from one place to another
preserved	stopped from going rotten
rebellion	to fight against rulers or people in control
sacrificed	killed as a religious offering
Scandinavia	Denmark, Sweden, Norway and Finland
scythes	tools with long curved blades used for cutting crops
tattooed	permanently inked into skin
taxes	money or goods paid to those in power
tunics	short dress-like clothing, with or without sleeves
wicker	material made of plaited willow twigs

Index

How to be a Celt

build a home on land... or water

make beautiful objects

barter your crafts

make a sacrifice

celebrate the festivals

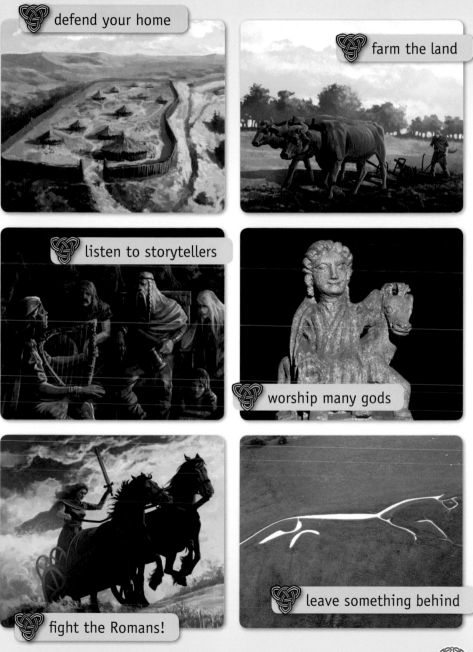

defend your home

farm the land

listen to storytellers

worship many gods

fight the Romans!

leave something behind

🐾 Ideas for reading 🐾

Written by Clare Dowdall ,PhD
Lecturer and Primary Literacy Consultant

Reading objectives:
- discuss understanding and explain the meaning of words in context
- ask questions to improve understanding
- retrieve and record information from non-fiction

Spoken language objectives:
- ask relevant questions to extend their understanding and knowledge

Curriculum links: History – the Iron Age; Geography – locational knowledge

Resources: materials for model making, art materials for jewellery design, ICT for research and presentation

Build a context for reading
- Ask children to look at the front cover and describe what they can see. Discuss who they think the Celts were, and what they know about them.
- Turn to the blurb. Read it aloud to the group and compare the information given to the children's ideas. Check that children understand the word "migrated".
- Ask children to imagine what Britain was like 2,000 years ago. Guide their thinking by asking questions: *What were homes made from? What did people eat? What was the environment like? How did people travel?*

Understand and apply reading strategies
- Read pp2–3 as a group. Discuss the information and help children to make sense of the map. Identify Italy and Greece in relation to Britain and relate this to the information given.